Trout Stream Therapy

Robert L. Hunt

The University of Wisconsin Press

A North Coast Book

The University of Wisconsin Press
2537 Daniels Street
Madison, Wisconsin 53718

3 Henrietta Street
London WC2E 8LU, England

5   4   3   2

Printed in Mexico

Illustrations by Ruth King, Tag Alder Creek Studios, Rt. 1, Box 280A, Sarona, WI 54870.

Library of Congress Cataloging-in-Publication Data
Hunt, Robert L. (Robert Leroy), 1933–
    Trout stream therapy
  Robert L. Hunt.
    84 p.   cm.
    Includes bibliographical references (p. 71) and index.
    ISBN 0-299-13890-9   ISBN 0-299-13894-1
    1. Fish habitat improvement—Middle West.   2. Trout—Middle West—
    Habitat.   I. Title.
  SH157.8.H83   1993
  639.9′7755—dc20   93-22106

In Dedication

This report is dedicated to Drs. Oscar Brynildson and Ray White, my mentors in regard to trout stream habitat improvement and my former fisheries research colleagues. They carried out several of the pioneering evaluations of trout habitat improvement projects in Wisconsin and formulated most of the guiding principles on which the present nationally acclaimed management program to improve living conditions for trout in streams is founded.

Contents

Contents

ACKNOWLEDGMENTS

Although no official record has been maintained of Wisconsin Department of Natural Resources personnel who have been credited with "inventing" several of the trout habitat improvement techniques reviewed in this report, there are key individuals to whom such special credit is due. These persons include: Robert Heding for the basic designs of the Wisconsin-style bank cover and current deflector structure and the half-log structure; Lester Peters for evolving the standardized, efficient, step-by-step process of installing bank covers and current deflectors; Jack Zimmerman for initial use of sandbags as a substitute for fieldstone; Terry Hupf for applications of GEOWEB and roadbase fiber mat; David Vetrano and Tilford Bagstad for devising the lunker structure; Max Johnson and Marvin Zadek for designing the skyhook bank cover; Robert Ostenson and his associates in the Northwest District Operations crew for perfecting the brush mat; Oscar Brynildson and Ray White for their promotion of benefits from removing woody streamside vegetation; David Paynter for first use of midchannel log pilings; Larry Stearns for the double half-log modification of the bank cover and current deflector; and Wayne Calhoun for design and construction of the first in-stream cattle guard structure.

Special appreciation is extended to Ruth Masloski King for creation of the artistic schematic illustrations of trout habitat improvement structures. I am also grateful to colleagues who generously provided original photos used in this report in addition to those from my own collection: Ed Avery, Wayne Calhoun, Elward Engle, Terry Hupf, Scott Ironside, Max Johnson, Roger Kerr, David Paynter, David Vetrano, and Ray White. If I have omitted anyone who contributed photos included in this report, the omission is unintentional.

Peer review outside the agency was provided by Richard Snyder, Pennsylvania Fish and Boat Commission, and Ray White, trout stream habitat specialist, Edmonds, Washington.

Appreciation is extended to Mark Lefebvre of Stanton and Lee Publishing Company for his assistance in screening potential publishing companies and providing the link to the University of Wisconsin Press.

Special thanks is also due to John Puelicher, retired chairman of the Marshall and Illsley Corporation, for his generous and essential financial assistance with publishing costs. His personal encouragement to me, offered as a fellow trout fisher and practitioner of trout stream therapy, was also critical in seeing the tedious publication process through to completion.

Technical review of the text within the Wisconsin DNR was provided by Lyle Christenson, my supervisor, and Ed Avery, my associate research biologist in the Cold Water Research Group.

Reprinting of this book in 2000 was made possible in part by generous financial subsidies contributed by J. Nash Williams and Friends of Wisconsin Trout Unlimited.

Trout Stream Therapy

INTRODUCTION

This manual has three primary objectives: (1) to help interested persons improve their recognition of environmental deficiencies that reduce trout carrying capacity of streams, (2) to inform them of field-tested techniques available to correct some of these deficiencies, and (3) to provide guidance, based on real applications, in selecting the most appropriate techniques to use—that is, those likely to have the greatest therapeutic value.

Because my professional, career-long involvement with habitat management in trout streams has been centered in Wisconsin, I have relied heavily on that background to prepare this manual. I am confident, however, on the basis of my professional travels throughout Midwest North America, that the techniques included are just as applicable in the other states and provinces of this region as they are in Wisconsin. Applicability also extends to trout streams, wherever they exist, that have physical and biological characteristics similar to those described.

Investigations to understand and beneficially manipulate biotic and abiotic factors that influence the number and size of trout in streams have been a continuous emphasis in the Wisconsin Department of Natural Resources fisheries management and fisheries research programs since the early 1950s. Several DNR technical publications issued since then, plus papers published in other scientific journals, have rigorously documented the evolving rationale for selecting candidate streams, described the variety of standardized, improved, and new techniques applied to achieve targeted objectives, and quantitatively summarized important physical and biological changes. A list of these reports is included in the References.

This publication is intended to augment that published scientific record with a report that emphasizes *a visual overview* of techniques presently applied by the Wisconsin DNR to protect, restore, and improve trout carrying capacity of the variety of trout streams in the state. This overview focuses on a series of artistic schematics of these techniques and photographs of field installation procedures and in-place structures. Brief narratives that emphasize construction and installation steps accompany the schematics and photos.

A few techniques, such as stream bank fencing and riprapping of eroded stream banks, are grouped in a gradient-independent category. Such techniques can be applied to streams throughout the range of gradients found in the Midwest region. Most of the trout streams in this region have gradients of less than 1 percent. Six therapies applicable to such streams are included in a "low- or moderate-gradient" category. Eight other techniques recommended for steeper-gradient streams are grouped under a "high-gradient" category, which spans the 1–3 percent range. Few trout streams in the region exceed this range of gradients over most of their length.

Following presentation of various techniques that can be used to increase carrying capacity of trout streams in the Midwest, some stream photo examples are offered of typical habitat management problems and suggested remedies. Twelve of the guiding principles that should undergird management of trout stream habitat are also included; these principles have essentially universal application wherever scientific management of trout streams is needed.

This manual is intended to be most helpful in providing biologically based guidance for proper selection, proper placement, and proper installation of the habitat management techniques described. Little guidance is offered regarding sizes of structures to build in relation to stream channel dimensions or stream flow regimes. Readers lacking knowledge of the physical sciences of geomorphology and hydrology are encouraged to seek consultative assistance from experts in these disciplines during the early planning stages of a proposed project. Nearly all stream rehabilitation projects will also require authorization by one or more governmental agencies. Appropriate approvals should be solicited early in the planning process for this necessary step too. In Wisconsin, for example, acquiring such agency authorizations should begin by contacting the DNR fisheries manager assigned to the county in which the stream of interest is located. Contact with this individual may also provide entrée to helpful technical and financial assistance.

Techniques Largely Independent of Stream Gradient

Stream Bank Fencing

Construction of a sturdy **fence** along one or both sides of trout streams to prevent access of domestic livestock is often one of the most effective managements that can be carried out to (1) preserve biotic integrity of stream reaches that are threatened by first-time access of livestock to the adjacent riparian zones, (2) hasten natural recovery of trout carrying capacity after livestock have been excluded, and (3) accelerate positive responses of trout populations in stream reaches where in-channel or stream bank structures have been installed to enhance carrying capacity.

Mecan River in central Wisconsin.

Buffer zones at least 3 rods wide are recommended on both sides of streams threatened by livestock. Use treated wood posts (with a minimum 6-inch diameter by 7-foot length) at corners, metal T-posts (6.5 feet) set at 1-rod intervals for line posts, and four tiers of barbed or woven wire. Corner angles of less than 90 degrees should be avoided so that livestock are not behaviorally "trapped." Inspection at least annually and after major flood events is essential to determine if follow-up maintenance is necessary.

A reach of Mt. Vernon Creek in southern Wisconsin shows severe damage from livestock (upper).

The same reach of stream 18 years later shows great improvement after cattle have been excluded by fencing (lower).

Cattle guard schematic.

In-Stream Cattle Guard

Where fences cross stream channels, in-stream, self-cleaning **cattle guards** can be substituted to prevent livestock from wandering up or down the channel. Such a cattle guard structure requires little or no maintenance, unlike a fence across the stream. Cattle guard structures are constructed of 1-inch-diameter black pipe cut into 63-inch sections, bent at one end, and welded to 2-inch by ½-inch flat, iron anchor plates. Space between the pipes should be 2–3 inches. Drill holes in the anchor plates so that 30-inch by ½-inch sections of reinforcement rod can be inserted to anchor the plates to the stream bottom. Weld washer caps to the top ends of the rods prior to installation as anchor pins. Install sections from bank to bank. Position sections so that the long-leg portions of the pipes are upstream—to enhance self-cleaning of stream-borne debris. Install signs warning people of an underwater obstruction if the stream reach is used by canoers or boaters.

Sections of a cattle guard structure in the process of being installed across a stream channel.

Riprap

Riprap is a simple and economical technique normally used to repair and stabilize eroding stream banks. Erosion-induced need for treatment with riprap is usually most severe along the outside current-bearing bends. Some channel narrowing and cover for trout are also provided in the riprap process. The larger and more irregular-shaped the rock used, the better. Quarried rock, therefore, has advantage over field-stone. Irregular, helter-skelter deposition is also recommended to increase cover for trout among the mix of deposited stones.

Most riprap projects in the Midwest are carried out along streams having erosion problems relating to agricultural land use in the watershed and riparian zone. Access to reaches of stream having badly eroded banks is usually good, even for heavy equipment and dump trucks, especially after the ground has been well frozen.

Under such conditions, use heavy equipment to slope the eroded banks to an approximate 30–45-degree profile. Dump truckloads of rock down the slope to create a base extending several feet out from the bank, and taper the riprap to the top of the bank edge. Partly cover the top edge of the riprapped bank with dirt to hasten recovery of more aesthetic appearances.

This severely eroding stream bank is a prime candidate for a riprap project, which will benefit both trout anglers and the landowner, who is losing valuable pasture land.

The riprap project in operation here could best be described as "dump and push," without any preliminary sloping of eroded stream banks. Inclusion of bank sloping is usually a site-by-site judgment call. Sloping increases project cost, but it usually reduces the degree of channel narrowing when riprap is added.

Natural vegetational succession has accomplished much to restore an aesthetic appearance to this stable riprapped reach of stream. When quarry rocks are used, as in this photo, cattle tend to shy away from grazing along the stream edge, because the stones make walking difficult for them.

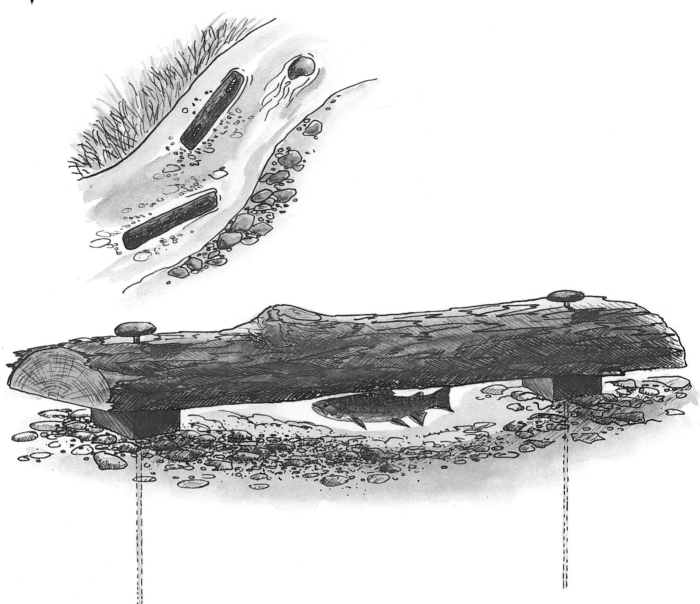

Half Log and Slab Log

Half logs and **slab logs**, both simple and economical structures, are used to provide resting and security cover for yearling and older trout in reaches of stream having sparse in-stream cover. These structures function best when installed on stable substrates.

Excellent sites include the margins of major flow concentrations in "runs" or "flat water" reaches and in or near the edges of pools; half logs and slab logs can also be tied in at the head or tail of good natural cover for adult trout, to extend the value of such sites.

To date, the most common material used for half logs is green-cut oak. Logs 8–10 feet long, cut longitudinally, provide two half logs. Width should exceed 1 foot, if possible. Bore ½-inch holes near the ends of each half log so that 6-foot lengths of ½-inch reinforcement rod (rebar) can be inserted through the holes and through spacer blocks about 6 inches square. The spacers hold the half log up off the stream bottom so trout can slip underneath.

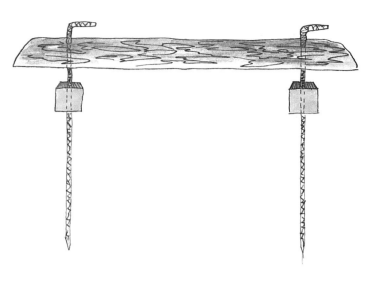

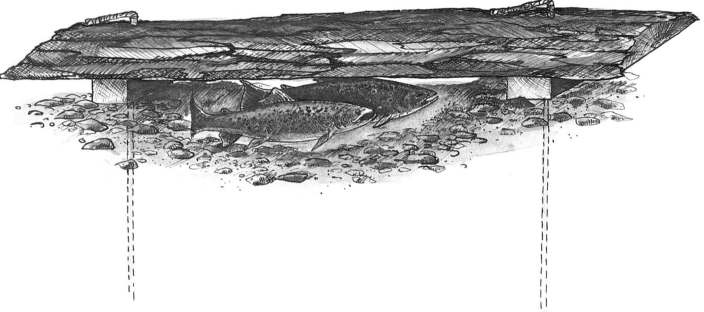

Position half logs almost parallel with stream flow so that low velocity flow is provided beneath the log. Drive rods into the bottom until about 6 inches of each rod still protrudes above the log. Bend the tips over in a downstream direction to anchor the log against the bottom. With a bit more work, anchor rods can be prepared prior to use with a welded washer cap on top and then pounded in flush with the log.

One common modification of the traditional half log technique is to substitute slab logs if such slabs can be obtained in adequate lengths and widths.

Slab logs, because they tend to be thinner, have special utility in providing midchannel cover in shallow reaches where trout spawn.

Whether half logs or slabs are used, the final product should be entirely submerged to retard rotting.

A typical half log about to be positioned (upper left). The near end of the log will be swung downstream nearly parallel to the flow before it is anchored.

Rebar anchor rods can be hammered into the substrate (as shown, upper right) or more easily driven in place with a fence-post driver slipped over the end. A practical feature of half logs is the ease with which one or both ends can be repositioned to improve performance after temporarily prying up one or both rebars.

A half log in place for three years over a gravel substrate (right). The shadow evident along the edge of the log indicates the presence of space beneath its entire length for trout to utilize.

Tree-Drop Deflector and Midchannel Deflectors

Tree-Drop Deflector

Combine polyethylene sandbags with deliberate **tree drops** to form quick and natural-looking deflectors of stream flow. Use sections of large trees, preferably dead or dying ones near the stream edge. Angle the portion of tree trunk used as a deflector downstream. Secure the butt end to the stream bank on the inside bend with a cable, or in-sert rebars through the trunk into the stream bottom. Place several sand-filled bags along the edges of the trunk to prevent undercutting by stream flow. Place one or two rows of sandbags on top of the trunk and cover with plugs of natural vegetation or field sod to enhance aesthetic appearance.

(See also photo on page 18.)

Midchannel Deflectors—Log Piling and Boulder Retard

Where substrate is easy to excavate, **log pilings** can be inverted and inserted into stream bed holes created with a water jet pump. Angle pilings slightly downstream and insert them deeply enough to keep the entire exposed portions beneath the water surface to reduce their tendency to act as debris collectors. Such current retards provide midchannel "pocket water" for trout to utilize temporarily when actively feeding. Boulders can also be strategically placed in midchannel to provide similar niches. (A partly completed bank cover and current deflector structure in the foreground provides more secure overhead cover for trout when desired—see pages 26–27).

A tree-drop and sandbag deflector one year after placement.

A cluster of log pilings provides additional feeding niches in midchannel for trout to utilize.

Large boulders have been added to create additional midchannel feeding sites for trout.

An excellent midchannel scour hole has developed around this installed boulder retard.

Techniques Recommended for Low- or Moderate-Gradient Streams

Stream Bank Debrushing, Brush Bundle and/or Brush Mat

Deliberate removal or drastic thinning of dense stands of woody vegetation began along the banks of small heavily shaded trout streams in Wisconsin in the early 1970s. The DNR instituted this procedure to initiate a series of changes in riparian zones and stream channels that would collectively bolster trout-carrying capacity and, secondarily, make such streams easier to fish. These changes include replacement of woody vegetation with stands of herbaceous vegetation more resistant to stream flow erosion along current-bearing banks. Consequently, better quality scour pools gradually develop beneath the hardy turf. Deeper, narrower stream channels also develop when herbaceous vegetation proliferates in response to increased sunlight and encroaches from the stream banks along shallow inside bends and along straight channel reaches. Within the channel a third benefit is attained by reducing shade canopy: greater growth of rooted aquatic plants that, in turn, stimulate increased production of trout food organisms and provide more in-stream cover for trout.

Tagatz Creek in central Wisconsin.

Brush bundle.

Potentially harmful warming of stream flow due to increased exposure to solar heating is a critical factor to consider on a site-by-site basis before woody shade canopy is removed. However, environmental conditions for trout in very cold, small streams may actually benefit if temperature regimes can be raised during the summer to increase the hours of water temperatures more favorable for trout growth.

The problem woody vegetation most commonly encountered along small trout streams in Wisconsin, and throughout the Midwest, is the inherently weak-limbed speckled alder. Initial removal efforts directed at such shade canopy consisted of cutting nearly 100 percent of the stems along both stream banks in 30-foot-deep strips. Healthy larger trees, if sparse in distribution, were bypassed.

Starting in the late 1970s and becoming quickly established as a standard practice thereafter, **stream bank debrushing** has tended to be less intensive. Removal of brushy shade canopy is emphasized only along current-bearing outside bends, where water depth is normally the deepest. Large healthy trees partly shading the stream channel are not cut.

Much of the cut brush is promptly put to good use in constructing **brush bundles.** Brush bundles vary in size, placement location, and design, but the most common procedure is to put them along the inside edges of bends, where deposition of stream-borne materials naturally occurs. Bundles placed here accelerate the deposition process and speed up establishment of stable encroaching banks that help to concentrate stream flow toward outside bends, deepen the stream channel, and increase undercut banks. Pools beneath undercut banks provide most of the hiding cover for adult trout in small streams.

Brush bundles placed along the shallow side of stream channels also provide additional temporary cover (4–5 years) for small trout and attachment structure for invertebrates.

One simple technique to create a brush bundle consists of placing three wooden stakes in a triangular configuration just at the tip of an inside bend. Each stake protrudes above the water 3–4 feet. Pile cut brush within the triangular area, with the butt ends toward the bank and the stems extending downstream. Lash several butts to-

gether with synthetic cord that will not rot away in a year or two and tie to the upstream stake. Tie anchoring cord across the brush from one of the lower stakes to the other to help consolidate the brush mass and provide additional stability.

If large dead or undesired trees have also been removed, anchor portions of the main trunks along the outside edges of brush bundles to provide longer functional life to the bundles and help deflect stream flow to outside bends.

Along excessively wide and shallow reaches of stream that tend to carry above-normal sediment loads, install

larger **brush mats** if enough cut brush is available. Such mats consist of interwoven, crisscrossed brushy material. Use a series of tie-down cords and stakes to compact and stabilize each mat. Brush mats, like their smaller brush bundle variants, help both to narrow and to deepen the stream channel and provide in-stream cover for trout.

Occasional (4–5 year frequency) refurbishing of brush bundles or brush mats is an option worth pursuing if sufficient near-stream material is available to cut, and where shallow water habitat for young trout is a high-priority need.

Brush mat.

A reach of stream in need of "debrushing" (upper left). Weak-limbed alders, weighed down by winter snow and ice, often fail to regain a vertical growth position. In their more horizontal aspect they act as debris and silt traps, destroying undercut bends, reducing stream channel depth, increasing channel width, and forcing the thalweg (maximum depth) toward the center of the channel, where cover for trout is usually sparse.

Initial cutting includes stream bank brush and any dead or dying trees near the stream edge that could fall naturally into the stream channel at angles that would degrade trout habitat quality (upper right). Felled trees can also be used to provide in-stream cover for trout after proper placement and anchoring (see Tree-drop deflector structure, p. 17).

Three stakes have been positioned on an inside bend (middle right) to form a triangular space in which to deposit cut brush to form a brush bundle. (The view is downstream.)

After the triangular space has been filled, synthetic cords are tied over the bundle to compress it and anchor it in place using the brace stakes as tie points (lower right).

24

Several brush bundles installed along the inside bend have trapped suspended and bedload sand and silt during the high flow stages, helping to narrow the stream channel and increase the undercutting erosive action of stream flow along the outside current-bearing bend. (The view is upstream.)

A mat of brush and conifer trees has been laid out along an extensive reach of this low-gradient stream to help narrow the channel through an old "beaver meadow." When dams are present and such meadows are covered with water, the soil chemistry changes, depressing the encroachment of natural woody vegetation for decades after the meadows are drained. Without deliberate remedial efforts the stream channel will remain excessively wide, shallow, and choked with organic sediment.

Twenty-six months after debrushing, aquatic vegetation has become established in response to greater exposure to sunlight, and stream banks are now well vegetated. An aesthetic marsh-meadow habitat characterizes the riparian zone. Lateral scour pools along the more erosion-resistant outside bends have increased in area and depth. Fishing conditions have also improved.

Bank Cover and Current Deflector

The dual-purpose **bank cover and current deflector** structure has evolved during the past 40 years to a place of preeminence among the variety of techniques used to improve trout streams in the Midwest. Several variations in construction procedures and materials have also evolved for differing stream conditions; but the basic design, purpose, and pattern of installation have persisted.

No other structure among the variety included in this manual provides as much simultaneous gain in pool habitat generally and particularly in that which is created beneath stable resting and security cover. The quality and quantity of these two environmental features (pool habitat and stable cover) frequently constitute the most important factors limiting abundance of adult trout in Midwest streams degraded by human activities associated with agriculture, silvaculture, and urbanization.

Begin in-stream construction by embedding pairs of 5-foot-long wooden pilings in the stream bottom along the outside bend. If the stream bed material is sand or gravel loose enough to allow it, as is often the case in midwestern streams, use a pressurized jet of water to bore a hole in the substrate for each piling. (See Lunker Structure, p. 40, if pilings can't be used).

Nail stringer planks of green-cut hardwood underwater to each pair of pilings at right angles from the natural stream bank. Next, nail green hardwood planks on top of the stringer planks and parallel with the natural stream bank to complete an underwater wooden platform. The width of

the platform will depend on the degree of stream channel narrowing that is desired. A width of 3–5 feet is common.

Place larger stones along the outside edge rather carefully to provide a solid wall. Cover the remainder of the platform with a mix of stones and dirt to build up a natural-appearing stream bank contoured to blend into the undisturbed natural bank profile. Top-dress with a mixture of regionally appropriate grass seeds, or field sod, or a combination of both. The new stream bank provides overhanging cover for adult trout to utilize in combination with adequate water depth.

Adequate depth is assured by building the structures sequentially along the contours of the current-bearing banks of the stream. Slightly overlap the downstream end of the one structure (its current deflector portion) and the upstream end of the next structure on the opposite side of the channel. Stream flow, confined by the artificially narrowed banks, scours a pool under most of the length of each structure. The flow is gently guided across the channel toward the next structure in an accentuated meander pattern. Newly

confined stream flow may also flush away deposits of sand and silt that cover gravel and rubble substrates. Exposure of these coarser bottom types subsequently provides more numerous and extensive spawning sites for trout and more productive habitat for many trout food organisms.

A high-pressure jet of water is employed to bore holes in the stream bottom for insertion of wood pilings. Paired sets of pilings are installed around the outside bend to establish the outline of the new artificial stream bank. (The view is upstream.)

Stringer boards of green-cut lumber are nailed underwater to the paired sets of pilings. Platform planks are then nailed on top of the stringer boards to complete the underwater shelf.

Mechanized equipment is utilized to deposit dirt and rock fill on top of the platform to build up a new stream bank. Larger rocks are hand-fitted into place along the outside edge of the new stream bank. A quarter-round strip of wood nailed to the leading edge of the sub-surface platform helps to keep the rocks from tipping into the stream channel. A topdressing of field sod and/or mixture of grass seed completes the new bank cover and current deflector structure.

After a few months of vegetative growth, a natural appearance has been restored. Deeper and longer pools along and under the platform-lined bends provide greatly improved trout carrying capacity. Anglers now have opportunities to fish almost continuously along one side of the stream or the other.

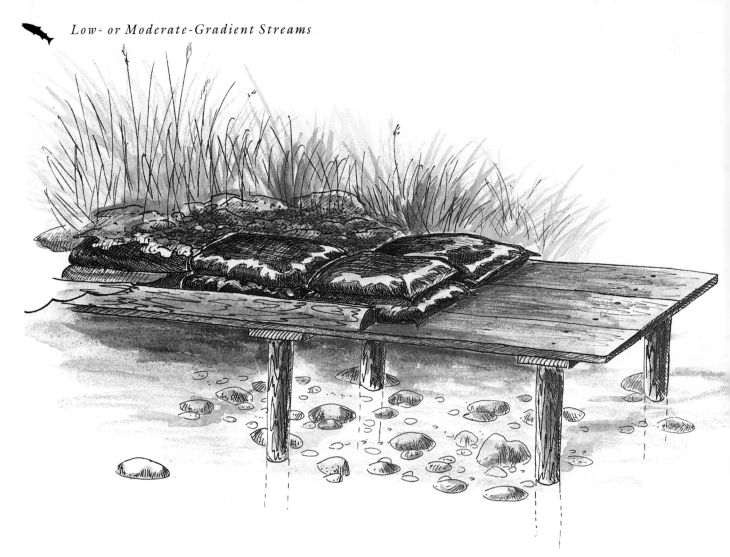

Sandbag Bank Cover

Where fieldstones or quarried rocks are not available, or they are difficult to transport to the stream, two substitute processes have been devised to build up new stream banks on the wooden platforms supported by pilings. One procedure utilizes polyethylene **sandbags** (16 inches by 29 inches) that are filled on site with stream bed materials and piled two rows deep and two rows high along the outside edges of the platforms. The bags and platforms are then covered with dirt and seeded, or covered with clumps of field sod.

Sandbags are filled on site with stream bed material.

After bags have been placed on top of the subsurface wood platform to build up and extend the stream bank, the bags are covered with chunks of sod, which have usually been dug nearby.

After one or two growing seasons, a completely natural appearance has been restored. Most anglers would not recognize that this stream bank is dependent on a wood and sandbag substructure.

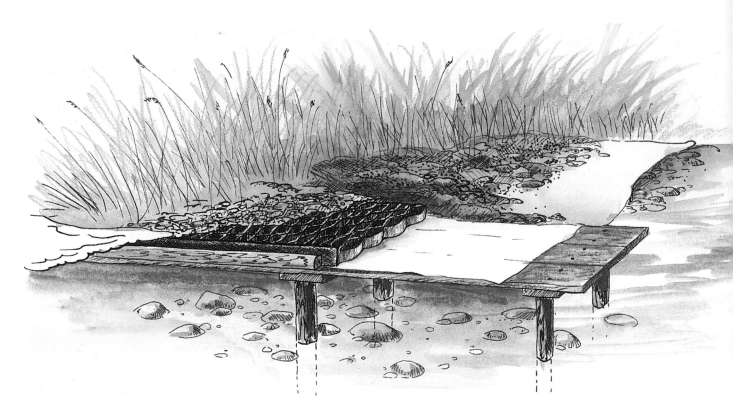

GEOWEB Bank Cover

The second procedure providing a substitute for rock involves the use of 8-foot by 4-foot by 8-inch polyethylene grids consisting of a series of honeycomb cells (commercially known as GEOWEB[1]). Once the grid has been anchored in place on a wooden platform, the cells are filled with stream bed material. Dirt, seed, or sod completes the artificial stream bank. To prevent erosion of cell material from the underside, a synthetic sheet of roadbase fiber mat is laid on the wooden platform to provide a water-resistant seal before **GEOWEB** grids are installed.

1. References made to this and other commercial products in this manual do not represent endorsement of such products by the author or the DNR.

An expanded polyethylene grid of GEOWEB showing the cell-like construction (upper left).

After the underwater platform for a new bank cover has been completed (upper right), the platform is covered with roadbase fiber mat (white material in background) to reduce water-action erosion from the underside of the platform, action that would erode away fill material in the GEOWEB cells. Pictured are several pieces of GEOWEB spread out and nailed in place over the fiber mat. Some of the cells have been filled with stream bed sand. Fiber mat is extended back and up the contour of the old stream bank and then covered over with dirt and sod to stabilize the bank and tie in a natural-looking contour profile between the old and new stream banks.

All cells of the installed section of GEOWEB have been filled and are ready to be top-dressed with field sod (lower left). Additional sections of GEOWEB must still be added on top of the wooden subsurface platform, which is visible upstream from the covered portion of the bank cover platform.

Several months into the postdevelopment period, natural growth of stream bank vegetation has camouflaged the synthetic material used to narrow the stream channel, deepen it, and accentuate its meandered pattern (lower right). The vastly greater amounts of under-bank cover that have been added, in combination with increased water depth, bolster trout carrying capacity.

Skyhook Bank Cover

The **skyhook bank cover** structure is another modification of the bank cover–current deflector structure pioneered in Wisconsin. It is designed for use in stream channels that are excessively wide and shallow and have erosion-resistant substrates and low-profile stream banks. The primary purpose of the structure is to increase greatly the amount of pool area and hiding cover for adult trout.

Use mechanized equipment to excavate a narrower, deeper, meandered channel within the boundaries of the existing channel. Install prefabricated wooden platforms along the outside curves of the new trench-like channel. Position the platforms so that a portion of each is cantilevered out 24–30 inches over the excavated trench. Cover the platforms with stream bed material excavated in the trenching process. Add the first material to the back half of the platforms to provide counterbalance weight. Sort out the larger excavated stones to line the front edge of the platforms. Apply a top dressing of grass seed or field sod. Restoration of a more natural appearance can also be hastened by planting plugs of natural grassy vegetation dug up from nearby stands.

Prefabricated skyhook platforms are stored and ready to use when the season for field work arrives.

A dry-land profile of a skyhook structure. The two-plank portion will provide the overhang of the new stream bank extension over the excavated trench. The back half of the structure will rest on the stream bottom. The vertical board will be positioned against the back-wall of the excavated trench. The section of limb (or more commonly a strip of quarter-round molding) nailed along the outer edge will prevent fill material from sliding off into the trench.

A series of stakes is pounded into place to provide a layout pattern for excavating a 3–4-foot-deep trench (upper left). Note the shallowness of water in the middle of this wide reach of cobble-armored stream. Low stream banks and an erosion-resistant substrate have prevented natural scouring processes from creating midchannel pools or lateral scour pools along the stream banks. Consequently, habitat preferred by adult trout is sparse, and fishing conditions are poor in such reaches. (The view is upstream.)

Trenching begins along the predetermined route, in essence forming a new, deeper, meandered channel within the existing wide and shallow channel (upper right).

Skyhook bank cover sections being unloaded and launched into the stream just upstream from an installation site (lower left).

A skyhook bank cover section being floated into position (lower right). Note the increased water depth where construction crew members stand in the excavated trench. The cover section will be floated to its proper location and submerged so that half its width will rest in shallow water and half will cantilever out over the trench, unsupported by any pilings.

Buckets of gravel and stones, dug from the trench and temporarily deposited nearby, are redeposited on top of the wooden platform to build up a new stream bank (upper left). In this photo, if the workman spreading substrate with his shovel were to step off the edge of the structure, he would step down into the 3–4-foot-deep trench.

Visible beneath the water is the outer log-covered edge of the submerged skyhook bank cover (upper right).

A strip of field sod has been added along the edge of the new stream bank (lower left). The remainder of the bank has been seeded. Occasional plugs of natural vegetation may also be planted to speed up restoration of stable stream bank vegetation. Barely visible in the stream channel is a series of large boulders placed there to provide midchannel feeding sites for trout to utilize.

Two years into the postconstruction period (lower right). A largely natural and much more productive reach of trout stream greets anglers and other outdoor recreational visitors. (The view is downstream.)

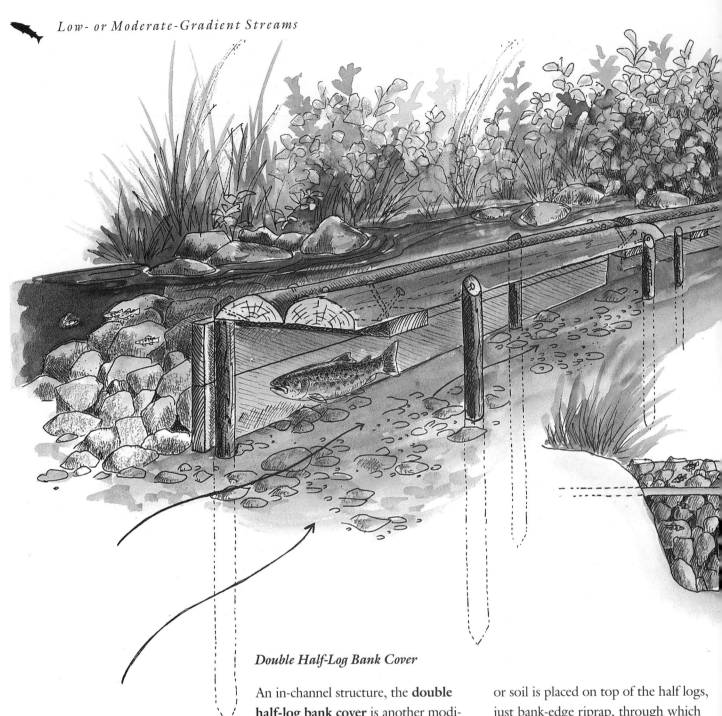

Double Half-Log Bank Cover

An in-channel structure, the **double half-log bank cover** is another modification of the Wisconsin-style bank cover and current deflector. All wooden components are installed so that they are underwater during normal flow periods. A vertical back-wall plank is incorporated into the platform to prevent riprap fill from tumbling into the stream beneath the double half-log bank cover shelf. No earth fill or soil is placed on top of the half logs, just bank-edge riprap, through which some stream flow passes. Even though this structure is positioned along the outside contour of stream bends (the deep side) principally to enhance carrying capacity for adult trout, it also provides good edge habitat for juvenile trout on the top side of the shelf (inset schematic above).

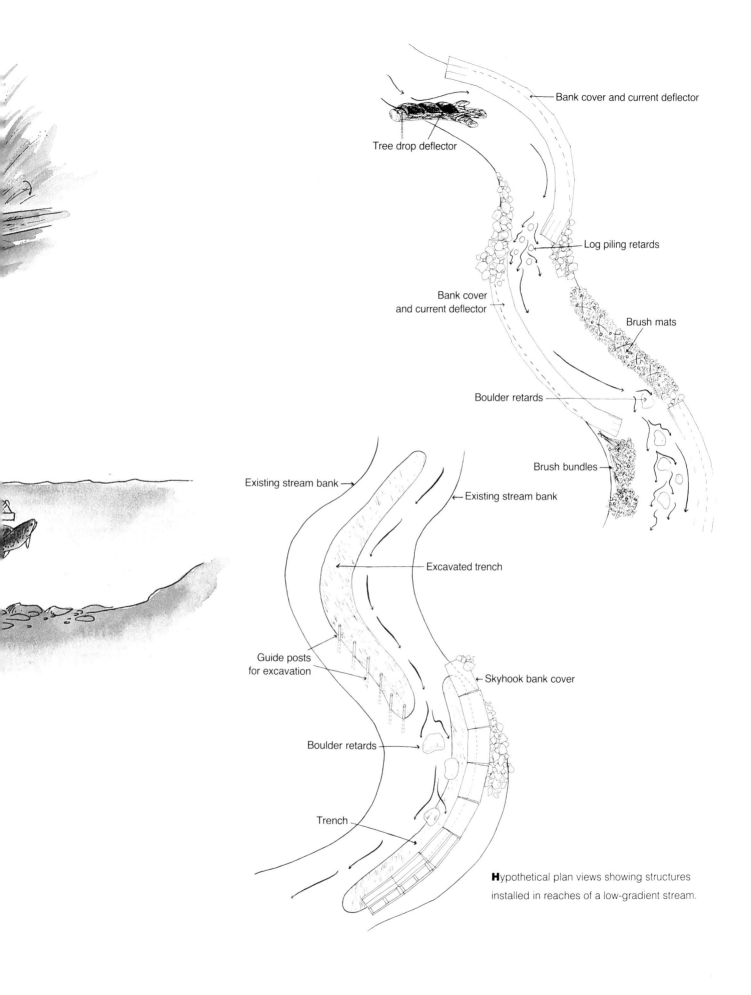

Bank cover and current deflector

Tree drop deflector

Log piling retards

Bank cover and current deflector

Brush mats

Boulder retards

Brush bundles

Existing stream bank

Existing stream bank

Excavated trench

Guide posts for excavation

Skyhook bank cover

Boulder retards

Trench

Hypothetical plan views showing structures installed in reaches of a low-gradient stream.

Techniques Recommended for High-Gradient Streams

Lunker Structure

The **lunker structure** is a modification of the bank cover and current deflector, designed specifically to increase the combination of pool and overhead cover habitat for adult trout in high-gradient streams that have extensive reaches of cobble and rubble substrates. In such armor-bottomed streams insertion of conventional wooden pilings is difficult. The trout habitat deficiencies and installation problems were simultaneously solved by designing a prefabricated, sandwich-like, wooden platform that rests directly on the stream bottom. Each platform is anchored in place by several rebars driven into the coarse substrate.

Camp Creek in southwestern Wisconsin.

Install structures in a continuous series along the current-bearing bends of the stream, or create additional structure-based bends if the natural frequency of meanders is sparse. Excavate some substrate material if necessary to submerge each platform completely at normal low flow. Use large stones along the stream-side edge of the platforms and smaller stones and dirt to fill in behind them. Slope back eroded stream bank reaches and contour to tie in with the bank of the lunker structure. Finish off with a mix of grass seed or sod.

This two-layer lunker structure has been assembled on site from 2–3-inch-thick green-cut oak. Note the six rebars positioned through holes drilled in the structure. When placed in the stream, it will rest directly on the cobble substrate. Trout find shelter in the 8–10-inch space between the upper and lower "sandwich" layers.

An overhead view of several sections of lunker structures joined along an outside bend (upper left). The two most upstream sections have been covered with quarry rock. The two exposed downstream sections will be similarly covered, and the water-exposed space behind the sections will be filled with rock too. Note the pattern of major threads of stream flow along the outer edge of the structure, bringing drifting food close to the structure under which the trout seek shelter and feeding niches.

Mechanized equipment is used to transport structures to the stream, apply rock and dirt cover, and slope back the banks (upper right). Sloped banks are commonly seeded with a mixture of bird's-foot trefoil, smooth brome, and tall fescue.

After planted or natural vegetation has grown for a year or two, aesthetic appearances are restored and erosion-resistant conditions are established (lower left). Gradually the exposed face rocks will also be camouflaged by encroaching vegetation. Note that the profile of the inside bend has been deliberately kept low so that much of the energy of floodstage flow is dissipated on the shallow side of the bend rather than against the bank cover structure around the outside bend.

Whole-Log Cover

Use large, crooked sections of **whole logs.** Pin them in midchannel or immediately adjacent to the main thread of flow. Position whole-log covers over gravel or cobble substrate where water is deep enough to cover the logs most of the time. Placement in or near the tails of pools and in runs of uniformly deep water is also recommended to increase resting and security cover for adult trout.

A whole-log cover placed in midchannel of a straight reach having sufficient depth to submerge the cover log (upper right).

A whole-log cover placed in a scour pool created by a K dam (lower right). Addition of the cover log enhances trout carrying capacity of the pool.

K Dam

The **K dam** structure is usually placed in straight reaches where obvious breaks in stream gradient occur. A midchannel scour pool is created below the structure, beneath the notched cross-channel log and ideally beneath downstream extension legs of the K.

Initial depth and dimensions of the scour pool can be dug, but periodic high stages of flow will determine long-term dimensions and depth.

Upstream brace logs are optional. If used, extend them well back into each stream bank at 45-degree angles from the cross-channel log. Armor ends of brace logs and the main cross-channel log with riprap.

Attach, roll out, and bury roadbase fiber mat or wire mesh (hog wire) covered with hardware cloth upstream from the main log, and cover it with heterogeneous substrate to prevent undercutting of the cross-channel log. Add enough fill on top of the matting to restore the natural bottom contour upstream from the sill.

A half log (shown in schematic) or a midchannel cover log can be added in or below the scour pool, if depth is adequate, to provide additional cover for trout.

K dam schematic.

A K dam soon after completion. The stream channel has been narrowed from about 11 feet to 5 feet across the splash log. The scour pool below the dam will become deeper after a few high-flow events. Good hiding cover for trout is already present under the splash log and beneath both lateral downstream logs bordering the scour pool.

Wedge dam schematic.

Wedge Dam

Install a **wedge dam** in the center of the channel in straight, high-gradient reaches just below obvious breaks in stream gradient through those reaches. The upstream configuration of the wedge will focus stream flow toward the center of the stream to dig out a plunge pool below the wedge and, ideally, under cover logs if these have been added along the sides of the plunge pool to enhance its trout-holding quality.

Join the two wedge logs at a 45-degree angle. Install the butt ends several inches higher than the apex junction so the stream flow will be concentrated in the center of the plunge pool during low flow and normal flow periods.

Attach roadbase fiber mat, or a combination of hog wire and hardware cloth, to the wedge logs. Extend the matting upstream, and bury it to prevent undercutting of the wedge. Adjust the height of the wedge so that a turbulent "bump" in normal flow is created over the wedge apex to help sustain a scouring action in the plunge pool.

Attach brace logs at a 90-degree angle to the wedge logs, and extend the brace logs well back into the stream banks in excavated trenches. Cover the brace logs and butt ends of the wedge logs with riprap. Give special emphasis to ample use of coarse riprap if the installation site does not have naturally high stream banks that will confine flood stage flows.

Initial depth and configuration of the plunge pool can be created by excavation after the wedge logs and brace logs are in place, but the long-term depth and pool area will be dependent on erosive forces exerted during periodic high-flow stages.

A wedge dam one year after installation. Good habitat for adult trout is provided in the scour pool and under the wedge logs.

Bank Cover Log and Current Deflector

The **bank cover log and current deflector** are a combination of structures designed to increase the quality and quantity of pools and overhead bank cover for adult trout; they can be used in straight reaches or at natural bends of high-gradient streams. Use rebar rods to pin bank cover logs in place along outside bends or against one bank in straight reaches. Partly notch out the underside of the bank cover logs prior to placement to increase under-log cover for trout. These simple structures can also be used without deflectors if stream flow is naturally focused toward them.

Where stream flow needs to be directed toward bank cover logs, install current deflectors on the opposite bank and slightly upstream from the logs. Care should be given to placement of current deflectors so that redirected flow does not strike the opposite bank upstream from the bank cover logs.

Riprap should be added behind the bank cover logs to enhance stream bank stability and reduce erosion.

GEOWEB can be incorporated into the wedge space of current deflectors to enhance long-term retention of cobble or rock fill, but this is optional. There is no clear evidence to date whether the addition of GEOWEB represents a substantial improvement over fill material that is shingled into place in a downstream pattern.

This bank cover log and current deflector combination is functioning as designed. After three years there has been little physical damage to the structures. Stream flow is below normal, but the deflector is still diverting a major portion of the low flow toward the bank to maximize its value in maintaining a lateral scour pool beneath the bank cover. (The view is downstream.)

A series of bank cover logs has substantially increased the carrying capacity of this reach of stream for adult trout. The single whole-log cover in midstream was cut to fit exactly between two boulders naturally present.

Channel Constrictor

A **channel constrictor** should be placed in straight reaches of stream channel that lack pool and cover habitat for adult trout. Use large, rough logs (20 inches or more in diameter), if available, for the two main face logs. These logs can be partly notched out to increase under-log cover for trout, or left in their natural form. The confined channel is pinched in at the downstream end of the channel constrictor to create a partial dam effect and deepen pool depth between the face logs.

Nail upstream brace logs at 45-degree angles to the face logs and extend them back 2–3 feet into stream bank trenches. Stabilize the ends of the brace logs with riprap.

Additional pool depth can be created by placing a large rock or two in midchannel below the structure (not shown).

Downstream view of a channel constrictor. Channel width is 10 feet at the upper end and 6 feet at the lower end. Cover for trout under the natural curves of both face logs is good along their entire lengths.

Downstream view of an excellent channel constrictor. It provides both good cover under the face logs and a pool between the logs that is much deeper than midchannel depth above or below the structure.

Cross-Channel Log and Revetment

A **cross-channel log and revetment** structure is excellent for installation at natural bends that lack pool area and underbank cover. This structure also works well just at the downstream end of obvious breaks in stream gradient (end of riffle) to provide additional cover and pool habitat.

Position revetment logs along current-bearing bends. Notch out to increase under-log cover for trout. Add riprap behind the revetment logs to improve bank stability. Install the shallow side of the cross-channel log several inches higher than the opposite end that junctions with the revetment log (see smaller cross-section inset schematic at left below). Partly bury and position the cross-channel log at a 30–60-degree down stream angle. This angle of deflection, plus the elevated tilt of the cross-channel log (see smaller overhead view inset schematic at right below), will concentrate flow toward the cover log regardless of flow stage. The maximum depth of the lateral scour pool is at the apex of the structure.

Attach roadbase fiber mat or hog wire and hardware cloth to the cross-channel log, extend it upstream for several feet, then bury it and cover with heterogeneous stream bed material to restore the natural gradient and prevent undercutting of the cross-channel log.

Reinforce both ends of the cross-channel log with protective riprap.

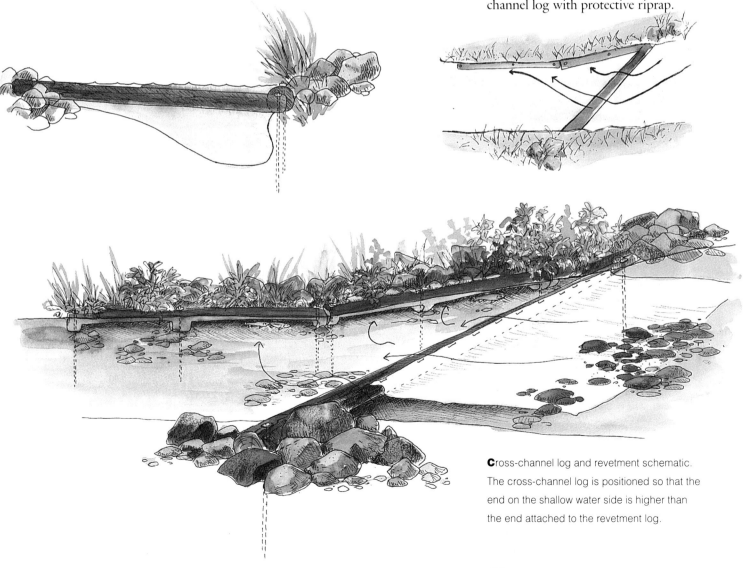

Cross-channel log and revetment schematic. The cross-channel log is positioned so that the end on the shallow water side is higher than the end attached to the revetment log.

An excellent cross-channel log and revetment structure functioning as designed. The structure is about two years old. A lateral scour pool has formed along the entire length of both revetment logs.

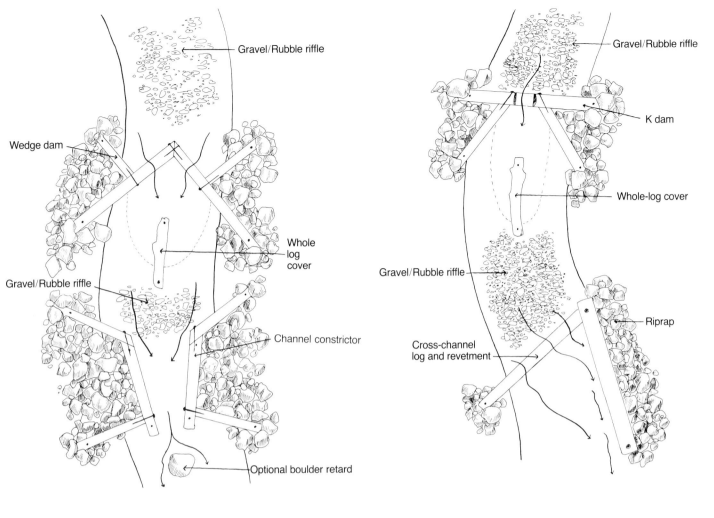

Gravel/Rubble riffle

Wedge dam

Whole log cover

Gravel/Rubble riffle

Channel constrictor

Optional boulder retard

Gravel/Rubble riffle

K dam

Whole-log cover

Gravel/Rubble riffle

Riprap

Cross-channel log and revetment

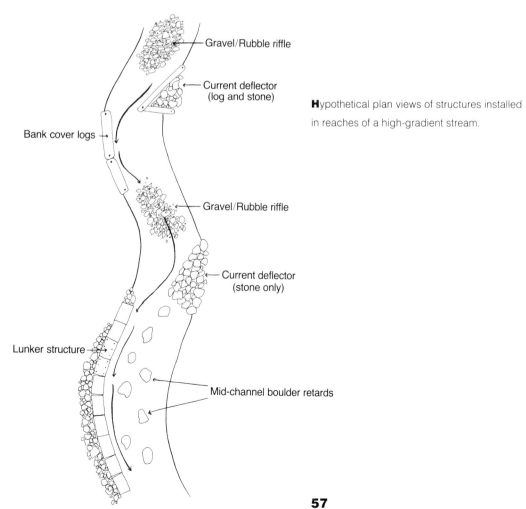

Gravel/Rubble riffle

Current deflector (log and stone)

Bank cover logs

Gravel/Rubble riffle

Current deflector (stone only)

Lunker structure

Mid-channel boulder retards

Hypothetical plan views of structures installed in reaches of a high-gradient stream.

Common Stream Habitat Ailments and Prescribed Remedies

Portions of midwestern trout streams, like those pictured and discussed below, need help to restore or increase their capacity to sustain good, fishable, wild populations of trout. Thanks to aggressive, persistent, and innovative efforts of professional fisheries managers and their skilled technicians during the past 40 years, effective remedies have been found to rehabilitate a variety of streams and trout habitat deficiencies. Examples of stream habitat management problems and suggested remedies are provided in the narrative text and visual record that follows.

Low- and Moderate-Gradient Streams (Gradient Less Than 1 Percent)

Unstable stream banks plague this reach of a moderate-gradient stream.

Remedy: Access along the stream is good for mechanized equipment. Slope back the eroded banks and add plenty of riprap. Use some rocks also to construct crude current deflectors positioned on inside bends to concentrate flow along the riprapped banks.

This pristine reach of moderate-gradient stream has a good diversity of high quality habitat, but carrying capacity for adult trout could be enhanced by providing more in-channel cover over the predominantly stable gravel and cobble bottom.

Remedy: Install half logs and slab logs to augment year-round cover provided by existing woody debris and stable undercut banks.

This stretch of moderate-gradient woodland stream has a good diversity of trout habitat—woody debris in shallow water for juvenile trout to use for cover, and scour pools along the outside bends for adult trout. Weak-limbed woody vegetation is not yet a major problem in terms of providing excessive shading, which would stunt growth of aquatic plants or weaken the physical integrity of stream banks, but attention will soon be needed to this threat.

Remedy: Remove the woody shade canopy along the outside bends only to preserve and restore a grassy turf and promote development of stable undercut banks over the scour pools. Install brush bundles along the shallow side to increase habitat preferred by juvenile trout.

Too much weak-limbed woody stream bank vegetation characterizes this portion of stream. Shade canopy during leaf out is also excessive. Stream banks have lost much of their undercut character and are starting to slump in and widen the channel.

Remedy: Remove most of the shade canopy from both stream banks and place brush bundles along the shallow side.

Excellent water quality and excellent recruitment of juvenile trout characterize this reach of low-gradient stream. What is lacking is permanent cover and pool habitat for adult trout. The stream channel is much too wide to concentrate the flow along the outer bends to create and maintain under-bank scour pools.

Remedy: Install bank cover and current deflector structures and half logs where gravel substrate is present. Additional gravel substrate suitable for spawning will be exposed when the channel is narrowed.

The stream channel of this low-gradient reach of woodland stream is much too wide and shallow. Cover and pools for adult trout are scarce. No midchannel cover exists along the thalweg.

Remedy: Intensive installation of bank cover and current deflector structures will be needed. Use fieldstone, if locally available, to build up new banks or substitute sandbags or GEOWEB. Narrow the channel by at least 50 percent. Add midchannel log pilings.

This stretch of low-gradient stream, impounded behind beaver dams for several years, is almost beyond reasonable rehabilitation. Stream banks have been largely destroyed. The widened channel and pools have filled with organic sediment. Little in-stream cover for trout remains. Water temperatures during the summer and winter approach lethal limits for brook trout.

Remedy: Remove any remnants of beaver dams to restore maximum gradient. Install brush bundles or conifer mats to reduce channel width. Depend on natural deposition of silt in mats and encroachment of natural vegetation to narrow and deepen the channel gradually and to restore meanders.

Damage due to beaver impoundments has been less severe. Most under-bank cover has been lost, but the stream banks are still largely vertical and channel width is almost normal.

Remedy: Maintain the reach so that it remains free of any new dams. Install brush bundles or conifer bundles. Whole-log covers could be submerged in some of the deeper pools to attract more adult trout.

High-Gradient Streams (Gradient Range of 1–3 Percent)

Unstable stream banks caused by occasional flash floods as well as annual snow melts exceeding bank-full stages have reduced the trout carrying capacity of this limestone-enriched stream far below its potential. A few deep scour holes are present. Natural reproduction is good in years when snow melt floods do not destroy developing embryos in redds or recently emerged fry. Trout growth is excellent in a food-rich environment.

Remedy: Install lunker structures or skyhook bank covers to provide stable year-round habitat for adult trout.

This high-gradient shallow reach is deficient in midchannel scour pools and lateral scour pools under the banks.

Remedy: Because the average channel width exceeds 25 feet, only the channel constrictor structure is recommended for straight reaches. At natural bends, use the combination of current deflectors and bank cover logs. Add riprap behind bank cover logs.

Shallow stretches of smaller high-gradient streams like these also provide little cover and pool habitat attractive to adult trout. Most of the water and space are going to waste in terms of providing good fishing water.

Remedy: Install in-channel structures designed for high-gradient streams. In straight, stair-stepped portions use channel constrictors, wedge dams, K dams, and whole-log covers. Where bends are present, use cross-channel log and revetment structures and current deflectors in combination with bank cover logs. Wedge dams and K dams would be especially suitable at the sharp breaks in gradient.

Nearly total destruction of all pool and cover habitat for adult trout has occurred in this portion of a small limestone stream. The riparian zone has been devastated by cattle.

Remedy: Use stream bank fencing and seeding to establish a buffer zone and filter strip along both banks. Let natural healing proceed for a year or two followed by installation of pool and cover-producing structures. Install channel constrictors, cross-channel log and revetment structures, and bank cover logs.

Good midchannel "pocket-water" pools for trout are common in this attractive reach of stream because of the natural deposition of boulders during glacier invasions. Edge habitat for trout of all sizes is also good along the undisturbed shoreline.

Management ("Remedy"): Stress preservation through watershed and water quality protection. Although it is arguable whether efforts to enhance the trout carrying capacity of this reach of stream would be worthwhile, it could be achieved by adding clusters of boulders here and there and some half logs in and along the natural runs of deep water, and by dropping a few conifer trees along the shore to provide additional habitat for juvenile and adult trout.

Some Guiding Principles for Management of Trout Habitat in Streams

Regardless of the choice of management procedures and enhancement techniques employed to improve or rejuvenate trout habitat in streams, project success is due to consistent adherence to several basic management principles. There are at least 12 such principles to keep in mind when formulating an administrative policy or philosophy for a program of trout habitat management, and to use as on-site guidelines when implementation plans are developed and carried out.

1. Learn from nature. What biotic and abiotic factors make locally "good" trout streams good? Attempts to restore the health of degraded streams should be based on local observations of the qualities of healthy streams.

2. Work with, not against, the inherent capacity of streams and watersheds to restore their biotic health.

3. Focus on identifying "limiting factors" at work in each candidate stream in need of renovation. Try to eliminate or ameliorate those factors that most severely depress trout carrying capacity, especially factors limiting the abundance of adult trout of interest to anglers.

4. Consider species-specific, age-specific, and season-specific requirements of the trout that are present, including both environmental suitability and social interactions with other fish species and age groups.

5. Tailor management activities to the individual stream. Do not use techniques just because they have been successful elsewhere, unless the streams are similar.

6. Disguise artificiality of manmade structures or modifications of the stream channel shape. Restore aesthetic conditions as quickly as possible.

7. Encourage the right kinds of stream bank vegetation to become dominant, depending on the character of the stream and riparian zone. Tough turf-building native species of sedges, grasses, and shrubs are normally preferred.

8. Preserve, restore, and accentuate the two most common natural characteristics of streams—the meandered channel and the riffle and pool sequence.

9. Make the stream flow work beneficially. Bring the main threads of flow close to resting and security cover preferred by adult trout, which is most often along the stream banks.

10. Whenever possible, maintain or enhance base flow (flow not augmented by surface runoff). Management of the riparian zone or entire watershed may be necessary to achieve greater and more stable base flow.

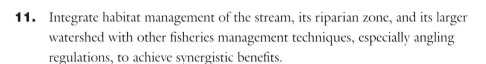

11. Integrate habitat management of the stream, its riparian zone, and its larger watershed with other fisheries management techniques, especially angling regulations, to achieve synergistic benefits.

12. Follow a logical sequence of habitat management steps. These steps should usually include:

   examination of pretreatment site several times during the year;

   diagnosis of limiting factors and their relative rank;

   prescription of remedies;

   planning, organization, and timetable to implement remedies;

   on-site treatment and development (the "field work" phase);

   quantitative evaluation of results achieved;

   inspection at least annually to detect structural damage due to floods or debris buildups;

   ongoing maintenance to preserve both natural appearance and functional performance of treatments applied.

References

This is a partial listing of technical literature relevant to trout stream habitat management in Wisconsin.

Claggett, L. 1990. Trout habitat development program review report—building a tradition. Wis. Dep. Nat. Resour., Bur. Fish Manage. Admin. Rep. No. 30. 27 pp.

Frankenberger, L. 1968. Effects of habitat management on trout in a portion of the Kinnickinnic River, St. Croix County, Wisconsin, Wis. Dep. Nat. Resour. Fish Manage. Rep. No. 22. 14 pp.

Frankenberger, L., and R. Fassbender. 1967. Evaluation of the effects of the habitat management program and the watershed planning program on the brown trout fishery in Bohemian Valley Creek, LaCrosse County. Wis. Dep. Nat. Resour. Fish Manage. Rep. No. 16. 19 pp.

Hunt, R. L. 1969. Effects of habitat alteration on production, standing crops and yield of brook trout in Lawrence Creek, Wisconsin. Pp. 281–312 in: Symposium on salmon and trout in streams. T. G. Northcote, ed. H. R. McMillan Lectures in Fisheries, Univ. of B.C., Vancouver. 388 pp.

Hunt, R. L. 1971. Responses of a brook trout population to habitat development in Lawrence Creek. Wis. Dep. Nat. Resour. Tech. Bull. No. 48. 35 pp.

Hunt, R. L. 1976. A long-term evaluation of trout habitat development and its relation to improving management-oriented research. Trans. Am. Fish. Soc. 105 (3): 361–64.

Hunt, R. L. 1978. Instream enhancement of trout habitat. Pp. 19–27 in: Proceedings of the National Symposium on Wild Trout Management. K. Hashagen, ed. Calif. Trout Inc., San Francisco. 69 pp.

Hunt, R. L. 1979. Removal of woody streambank vegetation to improve trout habitat. Wis. Dep. Nat. Resour. Tech. Bull. No. 115. 36 pp.

Hunt, R. L. 1982. An evaluation of half-logs to improve brown trout habitat in Emmons Creek, Wis. Dept. Nat. Resour. Res. Rep. No. 116. 8 pp.

Hunt, R. L. 1985. A follow-up assessment of removing woody streambank vegetation along two Wisconsin trout streams. Wis. Dep. Nat. Resour. Res. Rep. No. 137. 23 pp.

Hunt, R. L. 1986. An evaluation of brush bundles and half-logs to enhance carrying capacity of two brown trout streams. Pp. 31–62 in: Fifth Trout Stream Habitat Improvement Workshop. J. G. Miller, J. A. Arway, and R. F. Carline, eds. Lock Haven, Pa. 283 pp.

Hunt, R. L. 1988. A compendium of 45 trout stream habitat development evaluations in Wisconsin during 1953–85. Wis. Dep. Nat. Resour. Tech. Bull. 162. 80 pp.

Hunt, R. L. 1988. Management of riparian zones and stream channels to benefit fisheries. Pp. 54–58 in: Integrating Forest Management for Wildlife and Fish. U.S.D.A. Forest Service. Gen. Tech. NC-122. T. W. Hoekstra and J. Capp, eds. 63 pp.

Hunt, R. L. 1992. Evaluation of trout habitat improvement structures in three high gradient streams in Wisconsin. Wis. Dep. Nat. Resour. Tech. Bull. 179. 40 pp.

Klingbiel, J. H. 1981. The relative benefits of habitat development and trout stocking. Wis. Dep. Nat. Resour. Fish Manage. Admin. Rep. No. 10. 32 pp.

Les, B. L. 1980. Wisconsin trout stream habitat management. Wis. Dept. Nat. Resour. Manage. Publ. 600004D0302880. 5 pp.

Lowry, G. R. 1971. Effect of habitat alteration on brown trout in McKenzie Creek, Wisconsin. Wis. Dep. Nat. Resour. Res. Rep. No. 70. 27 pp.

O'Donnell, D. J., and C. W. Threinen. 1960. Fish habitat development. Wis. Conserv. Dep. Publ. No. 231. 15 pp.

White, R. J. 1972. Responses of trout populations to habitat change in Big Roche-a-Cri Creek, Wisconsin. Univ. of Wis., Madison. Ph.D. Dissertation. 278 pp.

White, R. J., and O. M. Brynildson. 1967. Guidelines for management of trout stream habitat in Wisconsin. Wis. Dep. Nat. Resour. Tech. Bull. No. 39. 64 pp.